Waves

Melina Gonzalez

BookLeaf
Publishing

India | USA | UK

Presentation by *BookLeaf Publishing*

Web: www.bookleafpub.com

E-mail: info@bookleafpub.com

ISBN : 9789357446969

First edition 2021

DEDICATION

For my daughter. My Alisia, my everything.

ACKNOWLEDGEMENT

I would like to thank my mother, without whom
I would not survive.

PREFACE

I have been writing poetry for years. I've never shared it with anyone, until now.

I'm Just Meli

You want to know me?
Fine.

I'm a mess
I'm poison
I destroy everything I touch
And sometimes I enjoy it
I have a lot of anger
I yell and scream and throw things
Because I'm dramatic
I have no patience for things I don't like

My anxiety is out of control
I am extremely high maintenance
I like attention and affection by the millions
But I don't like clinginess
The second I don't like something you do or say
I literally walk away

I'm nice to people until they don't deserve it
Then I'm a complete monster
With me it's all or nothing

I'm all about loyalty and honesty
The second I think you're being fake

I cut you off with no explanation

I'm incapable of happiness
Feelings are temporary
I'm selfish and spoiled and I plan to keep it that
way
And I will continue to be selfish and spoiled
And all the other things I want to be

If I were to tell you all my darkest secrets
Your image of me would completely shatter.

I am who I am
I say what I want
I do whatever I want
If that bothers anyone
Too bad
I don't care
I answer to no one

So, there you have it.
I'm Meli, nice to meet you.

Just the Darkness

There's more to you than just the darkness

You feed it
You let it grow
But there's more to you than just the darkness

You let it consume you
And swallow you whole
But there's more to you than just the darkness

There's a light in you
A kindness in your eyes
A reason to fight the darkness

Don't give up
Don't give in
Don't let it win
Because there's more to you than just the
darkness

Time of the Month

My flooding waves of depression
My monthly mental breakdowns
What good are they anyway?
Not like I'll do anything about it

You have too much to live for
You're still so young
It gets better

Their words mean nothing
The waves still keep flooding
The same waves I've known all my life

Sometimes I'm foolish enough
To believe I've won
Of course I've lost again

Familiar ocean sounds fill my ears
The waves I know too well
Come crashing in

But still
Not like I'll do anything about them

Separated

You hurt each other
More than you forgive
Too stubborn to apologize
Too loyal to walk away
Broken hearts
Broken spirits
This is not the family I know
Forced to pick a side
I choose what I know best
If neither side can work together
I choose to walk alone

Trauma

I never spoke about the virtue he stole from
between my legs
I never spoke about the precious gift he took
from inside my belly
I hid in the darkness of my inner thoughts
Afraid
What would people think?
What would they say?
Kept these secrets locked up tight
Not anymore
Slowly letting the air seep like a balloon
Before my head explodes
Some moments I feel like I can breathe again
Moments gone as quickly as they came
The nightmares come and go as they please
My demons dancing around my head
My thoughts and emotions
Their personal playthings
One day I hope to be free of this burden
Until then
I survive

How Could You?

How could you not tell me he yelled at you
When I screamed at you in his defense?

How could you not tell me he hit you
When I disappeared from your life?

How could you not tell me he assaulted you
When I laughed and told you to prove it?

How could you not tell me he hurt you
When I hurt you more than anyone you know?

How could you?
We're family.

You

When someone asked me what color your eyes
were
I hesitated
I couldn't remember
That's when I realized
I spent so much time looking past them
I was too busy trying to see you
The moment I realized
I had no idea what color your eyes were
That was the moment
I fell in love with you

Leave

There's a fire burning in my chest
Anger fills the air
Whirlwinds all around me
No more fear
Speak my truth
I don't love you
I never did

Your broken heart is not enough
I won't change my mind
I suffocated under your passion
Exhausted from the drama

I'm done here

Let me go
Let me be free
Let me explore the world unknown

You said you'd do anything for me
Let me breathe

Cautious

Love so strong
Breeds doubt
Too good to be true
I don't deserve this
How could I?
Happily never after

Could it be
Meant to be?
I believe it
Fight for it
Die for it

Always and forever
Happily ever after

Broken

Let's face it
I'm broken
No matter how I try to fix me
I'm broken
It's all your fault
If I never met you
I wouldn't be
Broken
But no
Because of you
I'm broken
It's all your fault
But
I don't blame you
Because I know
Without a doubt in my mind
If you came parading
Back into my broken life
I would love you with all the little pieces
Even if you don't love me back

Abuela

I can't stop crying
The world is blurry
I haven't smoked
But I'm hazy
Can't get my head straight
The day I've been preparing for
Since high school
That dreaded day
Is upon us
I miss you so much already
I never even got to say goodbye
I can't believe you're gone
The sweetest, happiest lady
I've ever had the privilege of knowing
Gone
Never forgotten
I'll never forget your smile
Your laugh
Everything you taught me
Always in my heart
I love you so much

Rant

Who says I have to choose
Between the club and the library?

Why can't I turn up on a Saturday night
And relax Sunday afternoon?

Why do I have to choose
Between lip gloss and combat boots?

Why?

What ever happened to being well rounded?
Why can't I be all of the above?
Or none of the above?

Stop trying to put me in a box
I promise you I won't fit
I am nothing you ever expected
A rare breed all my own
Individualized to my own preference

I am not your little doll
I don't break when I fall down
Trust me
I fall down a lot

But I lick my wounds and keep moving
Stronger and smarter than ever

You won't stop me now
Hidden away like Cinderella for too long
Who says I need a prince to save me?

I can save myself
As you can see
I already have

Something New

Day one
You're on a mission

Day two
You lost track in my eyes

Day three
You can't get enough

I feed into the attention
I play the game
Not realizing I'm playing myself

Caring
Considerate
Kind

Devil in your eyes
I play blind
My favorite adventure
Is that of true love

Caught me off guard
Opposite of everything I've ever known

Treat me like a person
Without erasing yourself

Funny
Smart
Dangerous

These are a few of my favorite things

Just the tip of the iceberg
So much to learn
So much to do
It feels right
Let's find out

One Day

One Day

I'm looking forward to it
When the name doesn't haunt me

One day

When I don't wake up in a cold sweat from the
nightmares
When I don't push away the people I love
I'm waiting for it

One day

When I'm comfortable in my own skin again
When I don't fear male genitalia
When I don't feel weak

Soon

When I feel like myself again
When I can stop crying at my reflection
When I forget what they did to me

I'm waiting for it

One Day

When the demons leave the crevices of my inner
sanctum
When I don't feel trapped inside my own mind
When I can enjoy life again

I'm reaching for it
I will be free

One day

Speechless

What do I say
When I have no words
How can I explain how I feel
When I'm so baffled by it all
Been through so much
And then
This happens
I feel
Disrespected
Betrayed
Exhausted
Angry
Upset
Hurt
Pain in my chest
So many questions
So few answers
What do I say
When I'm speechless

Writer's Block

Uninspired
Uninterested
Unnatural
I've lost my way
Too much to say
Try as I might
I have nothing to write
Unsure of what to do
Then I look at you
The words come flooding
Filling my mind
I take a deep breath
Put pen to paper
And hope for the best
You deserve nothing less

Cryptacrostic

Attached to my hip, your favorite spot
Just want to hold you in my arms forever
Looking into your eyes, my anti-anxiety
Only the privileged few see your face
If this is it for me, I know the true meaning of
happiness
Love is a word too underwhelming to describe
how I feel
Saved my life in more ways than one
Incredible how quickly I fell for you
Indescribable how much you mean to me
Nothing and no one can think to compare
Absolutely obsessed with your entire existence
All I have and all that I am, I live for you

Nightshade

I can't even say I tried my best
I didn't
I know where I went wrong
Everywhere
I didn't give you enough attention
I didn't play with you
I didn't talk to you
Or tell you I love you
Everyday like I was supposed to
I didn't call you by name
I missed your birthday
I didn't try my best
I screwed up
I with I could make it up to you
But it's too late now
I'm sorry
You deserved better
My beautiful Nightshade
Rest in peace
I love you

Thing One Fling Fun

Backless shirt
Sparkly short shorts
Six inch wedges
I'm ready
Newly single
And you're on my radar
You buy me a drink
Make it a double
Do that once
Then do it again
Brimming with liquid courage
Time to shoot some pool
I'm in your ear
"Don't mess up"
Pro turned amateur
I'm in your head
Game over
Side by side
I look at you
You look away
Good effort, but
I'm not looking for a gentleman tonight

I touch your arm
Your shoulder
Your hand
Suddenly, it happens
You kiss me and it's magic
The beginning of a beautiful friendship
With benefits

Ode to My Kids

My babies
You'll never know
How my heart shattered
When I left
You'll never know
How much I miss you
Little O
Little A
So beautiful
So loved
I haven't forgotten
Our precious memories
You're always on my mind
Every second of every day
I'm sorry for leaving you
You deserved better
I can't wait to see you again
Looking forward to it
The day we're reunited
I'll never leave you again
I promise
And the day
You get to meet her
I'll be complete
So here's to you

My first peek into motherhood
My heart
My babies
See you soon

To The Boy Who Thinks He Won

You think you won
Because I stopped fighting

You think you won
Because I left

The truth is
My victory has nothing to do with you

I won myself back
I regained and rebuilt myself
Despite your attempts to tear me down

So here's to the boy that writes his own narrative

The one that will tell all of his friends I'm a slob
Because I won't clean up after him

I'm lazy
Because I won't cook for him

To the boy that doesn't tell me my hair is a mess

Because he has "Enough problems
With men staring every time we go outside"

Here's to the boy that will tell everyone
I'm a liar and a cheater
Because I'm not a jerk to my male coworkers

To the boy who tries to dictate what I wear
Anything formfitting or slightly see-through
Automatically deeming me unfaithful, slutty, a
whore

To the boy who calls it
"The whole women's rights thing"

To the slut-shaming misogynist

To the boy who screams at me
Because he's logical, not emotional

The one who tells me I'm not better
Than all the women who cheated on him
Then raises his hands to me
Knowing I'm a survivor

To the boy who thinks I only say that
So I can play victim

To the boy who thinks

I only got an abortion
Because I couldn't "trap" him
Knowing I never wanted to be pregnant in the
first place

So here's to the boy
Who spent a year of my life
Making me feel unworthy of your presence

You can keep everything
Everything I bought you
Everything I taught you
And the life I built for us
You can keep it all

Because I got the only thing
I never knew I needed

Myself